Mighty Maxims
Anonymous
~*~

That's a good quote?

Explained in "An Interview with a Saint" my conversion from hedonism began with seeing an evil man leering back at me in my very own mirror. The first in an on-growing series of self-assessments, to help correct the problem I started searching the classic self-help books. -Tomes honored by a far more sustainable & civilized citizenry.

Finding the magic in many books – and like many – I found that some often fell open precisely where I needed to read. Humility. Sincerity. Matter.

Almost as interestingly sharing those experiences with others revealed much about my then-present set of "friends" – few wanted to hear inspiration any more than my evil mirror-man.

Onto something interesting, I began collecting the best of them. Quotations. -- When surrounded by vampires having a large collection of garlic is good?

Quotations, Anonymous

Of course I collected both attributed and anonymous quotations. Yet it was not until the onset of American Bidenism that I understood the need to share the best of them: "Sticks and stones might break our bones, but words'll make Liberals destroy you."

In short, whilst right-minded people can tolerate much from their opposite the reverse has proven to simply be impossible.

Thus it was only during our planet's logarithmic rise of Leftists that any logical being might ultimately understand the need for free-speech anonymity. QAnon.

P.S.

All anonymous quotations have authors. If you are able to attribute any of the following Mighty Maxims using any irrefutable, authoritative source then feel free to let me know!

Maxim #1: Anonymous

"Easy to use" is easy to say.

Maxim #2: Anonymous

"I must do something" will always solve more problems than "Something must be done."

Maxim #3: Anonymous

"They're not devils" she said "they're obedience challenged."

Maxim #4: Anonymous

"They're not liars" he said "they're truth challenged."

Maxim #5: Anonymous

'Pull yourself together' is seldom said to anyone who can.

Maxim #6: Anonymous

'Tis better to understand, than to be understood.

Maxim #7: Anonymous

'Tiz better to feed the sheep, than to antagonize the pigs.

Maxim #8: Anonymous

'Tiz better to tolerate their tongue, than to make 'em pull a trigger.

Maxim #9: Anonymous

'Ye needn't believe in God, too true. Nether need God believe, in you.

Maxim #10: Anonymous

(1) Everything depends. (2) Nothing is always. (3) Everything is sometimes.

Maxim #11: Anonymous

... so the system's crazier than the people that it's trying to help?

Maxim #12: Anonymous

A bad past is no excuse for a bad present.

Maxim #13: Anonymous

A bottle of sweat for every bottle of wine.

Maxim #14: Anonymous

A budget is just a method of worrying before you spend money, as well as afterward.

Maxim #15: Anonymous

A capeable freeman works not well as a slave yet the opposite is untrue.

Maxim #16: Anonymous

A carelessly planned project takes three times longer to complete than expected; a carefully planned project will only take twice as long.

Maxim #17: Anonymous

A celebrity is a person who is known for his well-knownness.

Maxim #18: Anonymous

A child of five could understand this! Fetch me a child of five.

Maxim #19: Anonymous

A clean limerick is a contradiction in terms.

Maxim #20: Anonymous

A close relative is one you see occasionally between family funerals.

Maxim #21: Anonymous

A crisis is when you can't say "Let's forget the whole thing."

Maxim #22: Anonymous

A crooked stick will have a crooked shadow.

Maxim #23: Anonymous

A diplomat is a man who can convince his wife she'd look stout in a fur coat.

Maxim #24: Anonymous

A fool and their money are soon 'Ponzied.

Maxim #25: Anonymous

A good leader inspires others with confidence in him; a great leader inspires them with confidence in themselves.

Maxim #26: Anonymous

A good marriage is like a casserole, only those responsible for it really know what goes in it.

Maxim #27: Anonymous

A good marriage winds up as a meeting of minds, which had better be pretty good to start with.

Maxim #28: Anonymous

A great deal of laziness of mind is called liberty of opinion.

> **Maxim #29: Anonymous**
>
> A great leader molds public opinion, a wise leader listens to it.

> **Maxim #30: Anonymous**
>
> A great nation is any mob of people which produces at least one honest man a century.

> **Maxim #31: Anonymous**
>
> A guy has to get fresh once in a while so the girl doesn't lose her confidence.

> **Maxim #32: Anonymous**
>
> A hunch is creativity trying to tell you something.

Maxim #33: Anonymous

A language that doesn't affect the way you think about programming is not worth knowing.

Maxim #34: Anonymous

A leader has been defined as one who knows the way, goes the way, and shows the way.

Maxim #35: Anonymous

A liberal is a socialist with a wife and two children.

Maxim #36: Anonymous

A life is like a tree -- if you don't make it straight when its young and green, you'll never do it when it's old and dry.

Maxim #37: Anonymous

A little nonsense now and then Is relished by the wisest men.

Maxim #38: Anonymous

A lot of good arguments are spoiled by some fool who knows what he is talking about.

Maxim #39: Anonymous

A man convinced against his will; is of the same opinion still.

Maxim #40: Anonymous

A man is known by the company he avoids.

Maxim #41: Anonymous

A man stands taller when he stoops for a child.

Maxim #42: Anonymous

A man wrapped up in himself makes a very small bundle.

Maxim #43: Anonymous

A mistake proves that at least someone stopped talking long enough to do something.

Maxim #44: Anonymous

A most important key to successful leadership is your ability to direct and challenge the very best that is in those whom you lead.

Maxim #45: Anonymous

A narrow mind and a wide mouth usually go together.

Maxim #46: Anonymous

A perfect wife is one who helps her husband with the dishes.

Maxim #47: Anonymous

A person is just about as big as the things that make them angry.

Maxim #48: Anonymous

A person who aims at nothing has a target he can't miss.

Maxim #49: Anonymous

A person who walks in another's tracks leaves no footprints.

Maxim #50: Anonymous

A person without a god is like a ship without a rudder.

Maxim #51: Anonymous

A present, over which you will shed tears of joy.

Maxim #52: Anonymous

A real person has two reasons for doing anything ... a good reason and the real reason.

Maxim #53: Anonymous

A smooth sea never made a skillful mariner.

Maxim #54: Anonymous

A spirit to find fault is an enemy to your peace and comfort. and also to the happiness of those around you. It is the key to your destruction.

Maxim #55: Anonymous

A strong person and a waterfall always channel their own path.

Maxim #56: Anonymous

A successful symposium depends on the ratio of meeting to eating.

Maxim #57: Anonymous

A user interface is like a joke: if you have to explain it, it's not that good.

Maxim #58: Anonymous

A vacation should be just long enough that you're boss misses you, and not long enough for him to discover how well he can get along without you.

Maxim #59: Anonymous

A vision without a task is but a dream. A task without a vision is drudgery. A vision with a task is the hope of the world.

Maxim #60: Anonymous

A well-used door needs no oil in its hinges.

Maxim #61: Anonymous

A wicked book cannot repent.

Maxim #62: Anonymous

A winner makes commitment. A loser makes promises.

Maxim #63: Anonymous

A wise man admits his weaknesses. I'd admit mine if I had any.

Maxim #64: Anonymous

A wish is a desire without an attempt.

Maxim #65: Anonymous

A witty saying proves nothing, but saying something pointless gets people's attention.

Maxim #66: Anonymous

A woman never knows what she really wants until she finds out what her husband cannot afford.

Maxim #67: Anonymous

A woman wears her tears like jewelry.

Maxim #68: Anonymous

ARTIFACT: The only true fact in an experiment.

Maxim #69: Anonymous

Act with kindness but do not expect gratitude.

Maxim #70: Anonymous

Action speaks louder than words but not nearly as often.

Maxim #71: Anonymous

After adding two weeks to the schedule for unexpected delays, add two more for the unexpected, unexpected delays.

Maxim #72: Anonymous

Air is water with holes in it.

Maxim #73: Anonymous

All I ask is a chance to prove that money can't make me happy.

Maxim #74: Anonymous

All diseases of the infidel.

Maxim #75: Anonymous

All gender aside, are you the next Mother Theresa?

Maxim #76: Anonymous

All great things are only a number of small things that have carefully been collected together.

> ### Maxim #77: Anonymous
> All happiness depends on a leisurely breakfast.

> ### Maxim #78: Anonymous
> All men have fears, but the Brave put down their fears and go forward. Sometimes to Death, but always to Victory.

> ### Maxim #79: Anonymous
> All those who are opposed to the plan I am about to propose will reply by saying "I resign."

> ### Maxim #80: Anonymous
> All work and no play makes one the wealthiest man in the cemetery.

Maxim #81: Anonymous

Always remember that you are unique. Just like everyone else.

Maxim #82: Anonymous

Always tell him he is handsome, especially if he is not.

Maxim #83: Anonymous

Am I ranting? I hope so. My ranting gets raves.

Maxim #84: Anonymous

America is a willingness of the heart.

Maxim #85: Anonymous

An atheist is a man who has no invisible means of support.

Maxim #86: Anonymous

An author ought to write for the youth of his own generation, the critics of the next, and the schoolmasters of ever afterwards.

Maxim #87: Anonymous

An error is the more dangerous in proportion to the degree of truth which it contains.

Maxim #88: Anonymous

An investment is anything that costs more than you can possibly afford.

Maxim #89: Anonymous

An obstacle is often an unrecognized opportunity.

Maxim #90: Anonymous

An optimist laughs to forget, a pessimist forgets to laugh.

Maxim #91: Anonymous

An ounce of application is worth a ton of abstraction.

Maxim #92: Anonymous

An ounce of intuition is worth a pound of tuition.

Maxim #93: Anonymous

And the joy of it all; when we count it all up; is found in the making of friends.

Maxim #94: Anonymous

And these shall go away into everlasting punishment: but the righteous into life eternal.

Maxim #95: Anonymous

Any simple idea will be worded in the most complicated way.

Maxim #96: Anonymous

Any simple problem can be made unsolvable if enough meetings are held to discuss it.

Maxim #97: Anonymous

Anybody who ask for advice nowadays just hasn't been listening.

Maxim #98: Anonymous

Anybody with money to burn will easily find someone to tend the fire.

Maxim #99: Anonymous

Anyone who thinks the sky is the limit, has limited imagination.

Maxim #100: Anonymous

Anything adjustable will sooner or later need adjustment.

Maxim #101: Anonymous

Anything is good if it's made of chocolate.

Maxim #102: Anonymous

Anything scarce is valuable; praise for example!

Maxim #103: Anonymous

Anything which is not directly observed tends to persist.

Maxim #104: Anonymous

Are we interested in sight seeing or soul saving?

Maxim #105: Anonymous

Are you interested in 'doing well' or doing Good?

Maxim #106: Anonymous

As a rule, a quitter isn't a very good beginner either.

Maxim #107: Anonymous

As every thread of gold is valuable, so is every moment of time.

Maxim #108: Anonymous

As our faith increases, so does our ability to obey.

> ## Maxim #109: Anonymous
> As to the idea that advertising motivates people, remember the Edsel.

> ## Maxim #110: Anonymous
> As you climb the ladder of success, check occasionally to make sure it is leaning against the right wall.

> ## Maxim #111: Anonymous
> As you grow older, you stand for more and fall for less.

> ## Maxim #112: Anonymous
> Attitude is a little thing that makes a big difference.

Maxim #113: Anonymous

Attitudes are contagious. Are yours worth catching?

Maxim #114: Anonymous

Auditors always reject a newsman's expense account with a bottom line divisible by 5 or 10.

Maxim #115: Anonymous

Avert misunderstanding by calm, poise, and balance.

Maxim #116: Anonymous

Be both the gardener and the rose.

Maxim #117: Anonymous

Be concise in your writing and talking, especially when giving instructions to others.

Maxim #118: Anonymous

Be different: conform.

Maxim #119: Anonymous

Be happy with the real pleasures in life.

Maxim #120: Anonymous

Be self-reliant and your success is assured.

Maxim #121: Anonymous

Be sure to save your money; you never know when it might be worth something again.

Maxim #122: Anonymous

Be the kind of person you would like to be with.

Maxim #123: Anonymous

Beauty seldom recommends one woman to another.

Maxim #124: Anonymous

Beauty without virtue is like a flower without perfume.

Maxim #125: Anonymous

Beck's Postulate: Murphy was an optimist.

Maxim #126: Anonymous

Bees are very busy souls They have no time for birth controls And that is why in times like these There are so many Sons of Bees.

Maxim #127: Anonymous

Before a man can wake up and find himself famous he has to wake up and find himself.

Maxim #128: Anonymous

Before the world finds a place for you, find a place for yourself in the world.

Maxim #129: Anonymous

Being alive is loving being alive.

Maxim #130: Anonymous

Being free of pretence does not mean you are in touch with the truth. Sincerity is not proof.

Maxim #131: Anonymous

Better aim at a star than shoot down a well; you'll hit higher.

Maxim #132: Anonymous

Better be upright with poverty than depraved with abundance.

Maxim #133: Anonymous

Better to live one day as a lion than 100 years as a lamb.

Maxim #134: Anonymous

Bizarreness is the essence of the exotic.

Maxim #135: Anonymous

Blessed are they who Go Around in Circles, for they Shall be Known as Wheels.

Maxim #136: Anonymous

Blessed is the person who can laugh at himself - he'll never cease to be amused.

Maxim #137: Anonymous

Both devils and saints aske 'why not?' - 'tiz only the saint who also asketh 'why?'

Maxim #138: Anonymous

Bradley's Bromide: If computers get too powerful, we can organize them into a committee - that will do them in.

Maxim #139: Anonymous

Breakdowns can create breakthroughs. Things fall apart so things can fall together.

Maxim #140: Anonymous

Breeding without licenses causes so many more problems than do unlicensed guns.

Maxim #141: Anonymous

Broad-mindedness, n.: The result of flattening high-mindedness out.

Maxim #142: Anonymous

Build bridges instead of walls and you will have a friend.

Maxim #143: Anonymous

Business is like a wheelbarrow - it stands still until someone pushes it.

Maxim #144: Anonymous

Business will continue to go where invited and remain where appreciated.

Maxim #145: Anonymous

But if a man happens to find himself ... he has a mansion which he can inhabit with dignity all the days of his life.

Maxim #146: Anonymous

But isn't hate just scorned love?

Maxim #147: Anonymous

By following the good, you learn to be good.

Maxim #148: Anonymous

Cahn's Axiom: When all else fails, read the instructions.

Maxim #149: Anonymous

Captain Penny's Law: You can fool all of the people some of the time, and some of the people all of the time, but you Can't Fool Mom.

Maxim #150: Anonymous

Caution is a most valuable asset in fishing, especially if you are the fish.

Maxim #151: Anonymous

Caution is not cowardly. Carelessness is not courage.

Maxim #152: Anonymous

Census Taker to Housewife: Did you ever have the measles, and, if so, how many?

Maxim #153: Anonymous

Charm is the ability to make someone think that both of you are quite wonderful.

Maxim #154: Anonymous

Cheerfulness greases the axles of the world.

Maxim #155: Anonymous

Cherish things while you still have them, before they're gone, and you realize how precious they really are.

Maxim #156: Anonymous

Chicken Little only has to be right once.

Maxim #157: Anonymous

Children are natural mimics who act like their parents despite every effort to teach them good manners.

Maxim #158: Anonymous

Children smile on the average 400 times/day; Adults: 15 times/day. Ever wonder why?

Maxim #159: Anonymous

Classified material is considered lost when it cannot be found.

Maxim #160: Anonymous

Clothes don't tell the character of the man, but they just as well talk for him as against him.

Maxim #161: Anonymous

Clowns wear a face that's painted intentionally on them so they appear to be happy or sad. What kind of mask are you wearing today?

Maxim #162: Anonymous

Common sense is seeing things as they are, and doing things as they should be done.

Maxim #163: Anonymous

Compassion sides more with all unborn than any sex-crazed executioners.

Maxim #164: Anonymous

Compromise: An amiable arrangement between husband and wife whereby they agree to let her have her own way.

Maxim #165: Anonymous

Computers are not intelligent. They only think they are.

Maxim #166: Anonymous

Computers can figure out all kinds of problems, except the things in the world that just don't add up.

Maxim #167: Anonymous

Conceit is a queer disease -- it makes everyone Sick except the person who has it.

Maxim #168: Anonymous

Concept, n.: Any "idea" for which an outside consultant billed you more than $25,000.

Maxim #169: Anonymous

Confidence is the companion of success.

Maxim #170: Anonymous

Consistency isn't a necessary aspect of life. The universe is unfinished, you know.

Maxim #171: Anonymous

Continue to be yourself because in the end that's what people will remember about you.

Maxim #172: Anonymous

Courage atrophies from lack of use.

Maxim #173: Anonymous

Courage is not the absence of fear, but the conquest of it.

Maxim #174: Anonymous

Courtship -- A man pursuing a woman until she catches him.

Maxim #175: Anonymous

Creative thinking is no substitute for hard work.

Maxim #176: Anonymous

Cricket is best described as organised loafing.

Maxim #177: Anonymous

Death and taxes may be certain, but we don't have to die every year.

Maxim #178: Anonymous

Death to all fanatics!

Maxim #179: Anonymous

Decisions not resolutions.

Maxim #180: Anonymous

Decisions terminate panic.

Maxim #181: Anonymous

Defendit numerus: There is safety in numbers.

Maxim #182: Anonymous

Democracy can learn some things from Communism: for example, when a Communist politician is through, he is through.

Maxim #183: Anonymous

Democrats give their worn-out clothes to those less fortunate. Republicans wear theirs.

Maxim #184: Anonymous

Desire for security keeps littleness little, and threatens the great with smallness.

Maxim #185: Anonymous

Did your mother have any children that lived?

Maxim #186: Anonymous

Difficult things take a long time, impossible things a little longer.

Maxim #187: Anonymous

Difficulties are stepping stones to success.

Maxim #188: Anonymous

Do it now. Then it's done.

Maxim #189: Anonymous

Do not clog intellect's sluices with knowledge of questionable uses.

Maxim #190: Anonymous

Do not follow where the path may lead. Go, instead, where there is no path and leave a trail.

Maxim #191: Anonymous

Do not look where you fell but where you slipped.

Maxim #192: Anonymous

Do not merely believe in miracles, rely on them.

Maxim #193: Anonymous

Do the thing you fear and the death of fear is certain.

Maxim #194: Anonymous

Do you realize that you are responsible for making this organization a cost, rather than a profit, center?

Maxim #195: Anonymous

Do your best to be the lead dog otherwise the view never changes.

Maxim #196: Anonymous

Documentation is the castor oil of programming. Managers know it must be good because the programmers hate it so much.

Maxim #197: Anonymous

Don't care if you'r rich or not, as long as you can live comfortably and have everything you want.

Maxim #198: Anonymous

Don't ask for a light load, but rather ask for a strong back.

Maxim #199: Anonymous

Don't be afraid to go out on a limb. That's where the fruit is.

Maxim #200: Anonymous

Don't be one to remember everything lent, but forget everything borrowed.

Maxim #201: Anonymous

Don't be too optimistic. The light at the end of the tunnel may be another train.

Maxim #202: Anonymous

Don't forget a person's greatest emotional need is to feel appreciated.

Maxim #203: Anonymous

Don't get yourself involved with persons or situations that can't bear inspection.

Maxim #204: Anonymous

Don't give other people a piece of your mind unless you can afford it.

Maxim #205: Anonymous

Don't just read scripture, study scripture.

Maxim #206: Anonymous

Don't overlook life's small joys while searching for the big ones.

Maxim #207: Anonymous

Don't start something you would be afraid to see finished.

Maxim #208: Anonymous

Don't tell me that worry doesn't do any good. I know better. The things I worry about don't happen.

Maxim #209: Anonymous

Don't wait for your ship to come in, swim out to it.

Maxim #210: Anonymous

Don't worry too much about what people think, because they seldom do.

Maxim #211: Anonymous

Drawing on my fine command of language, I said nothing.

Maxim #212: Anonymous

Dreams are free.

Maxim #213: Anonymous

Ducharm's Axiom: If you view your problem closely enough you will recognize   yourself as part of the problem.

Maxim #214: Anonymous

Each time we face our fear, we gain strength, courage, and confidence in the doing.

Maxim #215: Anonymous

Efficiency tends to deal with Things. Effectiveness tends to deal with People. We manage things, we lead people.

Maxim #216: Anonymous

Employed by cowards slaves fare better than freemen.

Maxim #217: Anonymous

Enjoy your life. If you don't, no one else will.

Maxim #218: Anonymous

Enthusiasm is contagious. You can start an epidemic.

Maxim #219: Anonymous

Every accomplishment starts with the decision to try.

Maxim #220: Anonymous

Every act is to be judged by the intention of the agent.

Maxim #221: Anonymous

Every beauty which is seen here below by persons of perception resembles more than anything else that celestial source from which we all are come.

Maxim #222: Anonymous

Every oak tree started out as a couple of nuts who decided to stand their ground.

Maxim #223: Anonymous

Every silver lining has a cloud around it.

Maxim #224: Anonymous

Every time history repeats itself the price goes up.

Maxim #225: Anonymous

Every time you lend money to a friend you damage his memory.

Maxim #226: Anonymous

Everybody has a hot button. Who is pushing yours? While you probably cannot control that person, you CAN control the way you react to them.

Maxim #227: Anonymous

Everybody's a self-made man, but only the successful ones are ever willing to admit it.

Maxim #228: Anonymous

Everyone has 20/20 hindsight.

Maxim #229: Anonymous

Everyone needs long-range goals if for no other reason than to keep from being frustrated by short-range failures.

Maxim #230: Anonymous

Everyone talks about apathy, but no one does anything about it.

Maxim #231: Anonymous

Everything in this life takes longer than you think except life itself.

Maxim #232: Anonymous

Everyting should be built top-down, except the first time.

Maxim #233: Anonymous

Experience is a dear teacher, but fools will learn from no other.

Maxim #234: Anonymous

Explaining the unknown by means of the unobservable is always a perilous business.

Maxim #235: Anonymous

Failure is more frequently from want of energy than want of capital.

Maxim #236: Anonymous

Failure is not the worst thing in the world -- the very worst is not to try.

> **Maxim #237: Anonymous**
>
> Faith is action.

> **Maxim #238: Anonymous**
>
> Faith is like electricity: You can't see it, but you can see the light.

> **Maxim #239: Anonymous**
>
> Faith is the vision of the heart; it sees God in the dark as well as in the day.

> **Maxim #240: Anonymous**
>
> Faith makes: The uplook good, the outlook bright, the future glorious.

Maxim #241: Anonymous

Few of us ever test our powers of deduction, except when filling out an income tax form.

Maxim #242: Anonymous

Finagle's Creed: Science is truth. Don't be misled by facts.

Maxim #243: Anonymous

Finagle's fourth Law: Once a job is fouled up, anything done to improve it only makes it worse.

Maxim #244: Anonymous

Find expression for a sorrow and it will become dear to you. Find expression for a joy, and you will intensify its ecstasy.

> **Maxim #245: Anonymous**
>
> First Rule of History: History doesn't repeat itself - historians merely repeat each other.

> **Maxim #246: Anonymous**
>
> Flying saucers on occasion   Show themselves to human eyes. Aliens fume, put off invasion   While they brand these tales as lies.

> **Maxim #247: Anonymous**
>
> For a man to truly understand rejection, he must first be ignored by a cat.

> **Maxim #248: Anonymous**
>
> Forgiveness requires Repentance. Repentance requires Remorse. Remorse requires Restoration, and promising to never do it again.

Maxim #249: Anonymous

Forgotten is forgiven.

Maxim #250: Anonymous

Fragrance clings to the hand that gives the rose.

Maxim #251: Anonymous

Friends are people you can be quiet with.

Maxim #252: Anonymous

Friends are those rare people who ask how you are and then wait to hear the answer.

Maxim #253: Anonymous

Friends are those who treat you kindly behind your back.

Maxim #254: Anonymous

Friendship is like a bank account. You can't continue to draw on it without making deposits.

Maxim #255: Anonymous

Friendship should be a responsibility, never an opportunity.

Maxim #256: anonymous

From Obama's "Dreamer" ploy to Biden's border invasion, knowingly undermining United States Law is the official definition of sedition.

Maxim #257: Anonymous

Frustration is when you have ulcers but still aren't a success.

Maxim #258: Anonymous

Funny, it is, to use the word "cool" to describe so many heading toward the opposite climate. --- Nyoda

Maxim #259: Anonymous

Genuine leaders know better than to ever define themselves as such.

Maxim #260: Anonymous

Gifting money to foreign nations is a fool's diplomacy. Deficit, doubly so.

Maxim #261: Anonymous

Give, and forget! Receive, and remember!

Maxim #262: Anonymous

Goals that are not written down are just wishes.

Maxim #263: Anonymous

God is offended in only two ways: We offend Him if we refuse to acknowledge His Hand in our lives and if we refuse to obey His Commandments.

Maxim #264: Anonymous

God knows that earnings are better than gifts.

Maxim #265: Anonymous

God supplies us with the opportunity, but He cannot take advantage of it for us.

Maxim #266: Anonymous

Good cooking takes time. If you are made to wait, it is to serve you better.

Maxim #267: Anonymous

Good decisions come from experience, and experience comes from bad decisions.

Maxim #268: Anonymous

Good habits are formed; bad habits we fall into.

Maxim #269: Anonymous

Good judgement comes from experience. And experience-well that comes from having bad judgement.

Maxim #270: Anonymous

Good judgement comes from experience. Experience comes from bad judgement.

Maxim #271: Anonymous

Goodness is beauty in the best estate.

Maxim #272: Anonymous

Govern thyself then you will be able to govern the world.

Maxim #273: Anonymous

Government lies, and newspapers lie, but in a democracy they are different lies.

Maxim #274: Anonymous

Governments last as long as the under-taxed can defend themselves from the over-taxed.

Maxim #275: Anonymous

Grace is harvested along the path to perfection.

Maxim #276: Anonymous

Greediness often defeats its own ends, by making us scratch for every trifle when we should dig for gold alone.

Maxim #277: Anonymous

Habit is a cable, we weave a thread of it each day, and it becomes so strong we cannot break it.

Maxim #278: Anonymous

Habit is the easiest way to be wrong again.

Maxim #279: Anonymous

Happiness is like jam. You can't spread even a little without getting some on yourself.

Maxim #280: Anonymous

Happiness is not always measured in smiles.

Maxim #281: Anonymous

Have a deep respect for the source of life and also for the ocean, for the forest, for the stars and for the truth.

Maxim #282: Anonymous

He alone is the happy man who has learned to extract happiness not from ideal conditions but from the actual conditions about him.

Maxim #283: Anonymous

He is a fool that praises himself and a madman that speaks ill of himself.

Maxim #284: Anonymous

He is truly wise who gains wisdom from another's mishap.

> ### Maxim #285: Anonymous
>
> He that loseth wealth, loseth much; he that loseth friends, loseth more; but he that loseth his spirit loseth all.

> ### Maxim #286: Anonymous
>
> He that will not command his thoughts will soon lose the command of his actions.

> ### Maxim #287: Anonymous
>
> He travels fastest who travels alone ... but he hasn't anything to do when he gets there.

> ### Maxim #288: Anonymous
>
> He was a modest, good-humored boy. It was Oxford that made him insufferable.

Maxim #289: Anonymous

He who ashamed of his poverty would be equally proud of his wealth.

Maxim #290: Anonymous

He who ceases to learn cannot adequately teach.

Maxim #291: Anonymous

He who dares to teach must never cease to learn.

Maxim #292: Anonymous

He who has burned his mouth blows his soup.

Maxim #293: Anonymous

He who lives without folly is less wise than he believes.

Maxim #294: Anonymous

He who prides himself upon wealth and honor hastens his own downfall.

Maxim #295: Anonymous

He who puts his hand to the plow and looks back is not fit for the kingdom of winners.

Maxim #296: Anonymous

He who steals for others ends up being hanged for himself.

Maxim #297: Anonymous

He who thinks by the inch and talks by the yard deserves to be kicked by the foot.

Maxim #298: Anonymous

He who throws dirt always loses ground.

Maxim #299: Anonymous

He whom God would destroy, He first makes insane.

Maxim #300: Anonymous

He's just a politician trying to save both his faces ...

Maxim #301: Anonymous

He's the kind of a guy who lights up a room just by flicking a switch.

Maxim #302: Anonymous

Hear much, speak little.

Maxim #303: Anonymous

Help your enemy today! It'll drive them CrAzY!

Maxim #304: Anonymous

Here comes the orator, with his flood of words and his drop of reason.

Maxim #305: Anonymous

Hire the teenager while they still know everything!

Maxim #306: Anonymous

His life was a sort of dream, as are most lives with the mainspring left out.

Maxim #307: Anonymous

Hold a good friend in both your hands.

Maxim #308: Anonymous

Homosexuality is not hereditary.

Maxim #309: Anonymous

Hoping and waiting is not by way of doing things.

Maxim #310: Anonymous

Horngren's Observation: Among economists, the real world is often a special case.

Maxim #311: Anonymous

How can you work when the system's so crowded?

Maxim #312: Anonymous

Hummingbirds never remember the words to songs.

Maxim #313: Anonymous

Humor is a whisper from the soul, imploring mind and body to relax, let go and be at peace again.

Maxim #314: Anonymous

Hyperpolysyllabicomania is a fondness for big words.

Maxim #315: Anonymous

I am today what yesterday has made me - Tomorrow I shall be changed by today's experiences.

Maxim #316: Anonymous

I bit my tongue and stood in line With not much to believe in I bought into what I was sold And ended up with nothing.

Maxim #317: Anonymous

I can alter my life by altering the attitude of my mind.

Maxim #318: Anonymous

I don't know about you, but my parents are always right.

Maxim #319: Anonymous

I don't know whether to keep silent and let people think I am ignorant or open my mouth and release all doubts.

Maxim #320: Anonymous

I don't pay you for brilliant code, I pay you for maintainable code.

Maxim #321: Anonymous

I don't understand the need countries have to be importing poverty. -Don't they have enough of it already?

Maxim #322: Anonymous

I get frustrated doing twice as much work so protected groups can stand around and ridicule me. Its like a sick joke at this point.

Maxim #323: Anonymous

I have a C program that has been running on UNIX, unchanged, since 1978!

Maxim #324: Anonymous

I have read many books, but the Bible reads me.

Maxim #325: Anonymous

I knew a kenyan dude who always told me to work hard, "enjoy now and suffer later, or suffer now and enjoy later."

Maxim #326: Anonymous

I like your game but we have to change the rules.

Maxim #327: Anonymous

I told my wife that a husband is like a fine wine; he gets better with age. The next day, she locked me in the cellar.

Maxim #328: Anonymous

I was born to fight your brand of order!   - The Adventures of Batman & Robin.

Maxim #329: Anonymous

I was unable to stop in time and my car crashed into the other vehicle. The driver and passengers then left for a vacation with injuries.

Maxim #330: Anonymous

I'd rather look forward and dream, then look backwards and regret.

Maxim #331: Anonymous

I'm #1! Why try harder?

Maxim #332: Anonymous

I'm a creationist; I refuse to believe that I could have evolved from man.

Maxim #333: Anonymous

I'm prepared for all emergencies but totally unprepared for everyday life.

Maxim #334: Anonymous

I've tried relaxing, but - I don't know - I feel more comfortable tense.

Maxim #335: Anonymous

If all men told the truth, the tears of the women would create another flood.

Maxim #336: Anonymous

If all of our wishes were gratified, many of our dreams would be destroyed.

Maxim #337: Anonymous

If an apparently severe problem manifests itself, no solution is acceptable unless it is involved, expensive, and time-consuming.

Maxim #338: Anonymous

If anyone accepts my help who doesn't need it, that's his problem; if I refuse my help to anyone who needs it, that's my problem.

Maxim #339: Anonymous

If at first you don't succeed, you'll get a lot of free advice from folks who didn't succeed either.

Maxim #340: Anonymous

If everybody's thinking alike, somebody isn't thinking.

Maxim #341: Anonymous

If happiness could be brought, few of us could pay the price.

Maxim #342: Anonymous

If hard work is the greatest thing on Earth, I'll try Mars.

Maxim #343: Anonymous

If humanity profits from its mistakes, we have a glorious future coming up.

Maxim #344: Anonymous

If ignorance is bliss, why aren't more people jumping up and down for joy.

Maxim #345: Anonymous

If it ain't broke don't fix it.

Maxim #346: Anonymous

If it succeeds, it is right; if it fails, it is wrong.

Maxim #347: Anonymous

If it wasn't for the last minute, nothing would get done.

Maxim #348: Anonymous

If it weren't for caffeine I'd have no personality whatsoever!

Maxim #349: Anonymous

If it weren't for the last minute, nothing would get done.

Maxim #350: Anonymous

If life were a bed of roses, some people wouldn't be happy until they developed an allergy.

Maxim #351: Anonymous

If man cannot face what he is, then man cannot be free.

Maxim #352: Anonymous

If one knows what the task is, and there is a time limit allowed for the completion of the task, then one cannot guess how much it will cost.

Maxim #353: Anonymous

If one word does not succeed, ten thousand are of no avail.

Maxim #354: Anonymous

If only one could get that wonderful feeling of accomplishment without having to accomplish anything.

Maxim #355: Anonymous

If pro is the opposite of con, is Progress the opposite of Congress?

Maxim #356: Anonymous

If the going is real easy, beware, you may be headed down-hill, and don't know it.

Maxim #357: Anonymous

If the truth be known, most successes are built on a multitude of failures.

Maxim #358: Anonymous

If there is anything better than to be loved it is loving.

Maxim #359: Anonymous

If things were left to chance, they'd be better.

Maxim #360: Anonymous

If we are learning to simply get a job, learning stops once we have one.

Maxim #361: Anonymous

If we don't get some money in our bank account soon, we'll be arrested for impersonating the government.

Maxim #362: Anonymous

If we don't take care of the customer, somebody else will.

Maxim #363: Anonymous

If we ever knew exactly where the light was coming from, getting there would be easy.

Maxim #364: Anonymous

If you are all wrapped up in yourself, you are overdressed. If you are all wrapped up in yourself, you make a very small package.

> **Maxim #365: Anonymous**
>
> If you are concerned about being criticized, you're in the wrong job.

> **Maxim #366: Anonymous**
>
> If you are right, take the humble side -- you will help the other fellow. If you are wrong, take the humble side -- and you will help yourself.

> **Maxim #367: Anonymous**
>
> If you aren't in over your head, how do you know how tall you are?

> **Maxim #368: Anonymous**
>
> If you can't do anything about something, pretend it doesn't exist.

Maxim #369: Anonymous

If you can't do what you're requiring of others, don't expect their respect.

Maxim #370: Anonymous

If you cry because the sun has gone out of your life, your tears will prevent you from seeing the stars.

Maxim #371: Anonymous

If you don't climb the mountain, you can't view the plain.

Maxim #372: Anonymous

If you don't have time to do it right you must have time to do it over.

> **Maxim #373: Anonymous**
>
> If you fear nothing, you love nothing. If you love nothing, what joy can there be in life?

> **Maxim #374: Anonymous**
>
> If you get up one time more than you fall, you will make it through.

> **Maxim #375: Anonymous**
>
> If you had it all to do over, would you fall in love with yourself again?

> **Maxim #376: Anonymous**
>
> If you have to shoot, shoot. Don't talk.

Maxim #377: Anonymous

If you like the post office, you are going to LOVE national health care.

Maxim #378: Anonymous

If you look back too much, you will soon be headed that way.

Maxim #379: Anonymous

If you stand up to be counted, someone will take your seat.

Maxim #380: Anonymous

If you start soon enough, you won't have to run to catch up.

Maxim #381: Anonymous

If you take pleasure in criticism, it's time to hold you tongue.

Maxim #382: Anonymous

If you talk about someone behind their back, their back will be right behind you.

Maxim #383: Anonymous

If you want a blest, not devil's life. Then do not heed, the lift's advice.

Maxim #384: Anonymous

If you want to be somebody, somebody really special, be yourself.

Maxim #385: Anonymous

If you want to be successful, you must either have a chance or take one.

Maxim #386: Anonymous

If you want to get something done, give it to a busy person.

Maxim #387: Anonymous

If you want to launch big ships you have to go where the water is deep.

Maxim #388: Anonymous

If you want to manage somebody, manage yourself. Do that well and you'll be ready to stop managing. And start leading.

Maxim #389: Anonymous

If you want your spouse to listen and pay strict attention to every word you say, talk in your sleep.

Maxim #390: Anonymous

If you wish, you will have an opportunity.

Maxim #391: Anonymous

If you work on a nonexistent problem there are much fewer obstacles to overcome.

Maxim #392: Anonymous

If you would attain greatness, think no little thoughts.

Maxim #393: Anonymous

If you're too busy to help those around you succeed, you're too busy.

Maxim #394: Anonymous

If you've enjoyed a little and endured a lot, you've really done pretty well.

Maxim #395: Anonymous

If your knees are knocking, kneel on them.

Maxim #396: Anonymous

If your life is free of failures, you're not taking enough risks.

Maxim #397: Anonymous

If your subordinates are not making an occasional mistake or two, it is a sure sign they are playing it too safe.

Maxim #398: Anonymous

If your sword's too short, add to its length by taking one step forward.

Maxim #399: Anonymous

Ignorance is no excuse.

Maxim #400: Anonymous

Immortality lies not in the things you leave behind, but in the people your life has touched.

Maxim #401: Anonymous

In a real dark night of the soul it is always three o clock in the morning. day after day.

Maxim #402: Anonymous

In a war of ideas, it is people who get killed.

Maxim #403: Anonymous

In a world full of people we are alone.

Maxim #404: Anonymous

In a world where the outrageous has become the norm, stable organizations make no sense.

Maxim #405: Anonymous

In order for you to profit from your mistakes, you have to get out and make some.

Maxim #406: Anonymous

In order to get from what was to what will be, you must go through what is.

Maxim #407: Anonymous

In order to succeed, you must first be willing to fail.

Maxim #408: Anonymous

In order to win $100.00 in a $2 lottery, at least 50 people must loose. Your lucky numbers are 100, 2, and 51.

Maxim #409: Anonymous

In the land of the blind, the one-eyed man is insane.

Maxim #410: Anonymous

Inflation is when sitting on your nest egg doesn't give you anything to crow about.

Maxim #411: Anonymous

Insecurity exists in the absence of knowledge.

Maxim #412: Anonymous

Institute: An archaic school where football in not taught.

Maxim #413: Anonymous

Intuition: going your way without inquiring about the way.

Maxim #414: Anonymous

Is any punishment too severe? For those who corrupt our children, dear? Hung by their necks until they're dead? - One sure path to progress, ahead!

Maxim #415: Anonymous

It has just been discovered that research causes cancer in rats.

Maxim #416: Anonymous

It is a wise person that adapts themselves to all contingencies; it's the fool who always struggles like a swimmer against the current.

Maxim #417: Anonymous

It is better to ask twice than to lose your way once.

Maxim #418: Anonymous

It is better to have loved and lost than just to have lost.

Maxim #419: Anonymous

It is customary for a decimal to be misplaced.

Maxim #420: Anonymous

It is easier to change the specification to fit the program than vice versa.

Maxim #421: Anonymous

It is easier to harness human nature than to fight or repress it.

Maxim #422: Anonymous

It is easier to write an incorrect program than understand a correct one.

Maxim #423: Anonymous

It is in the nature of mobs to cheer fools.

Maxim #424: Anonymous

It is kind of happiness to know to what extent we may be unhappy.

Maxim #425: Anonymous

It is much easier for good to deal with evil than it is for good to deal with stupidity.

Maxim #426: Anonymous

It is no pleasure to build a web and catch only flies when one knows there is a wasp about.

Maxim #427: Anonymous

It is not important what you believe, only that you believe.

Maxim #428: Anonymous

It is now beyond any doubt that cigarettes are the biggest cause of statistics.

Maxim #429: Anonymous

It is said that only a fool learns from his own mistakes, a wise man from the mistakes of others.

Maxim #430: Anonymous

It is the pleasure of reward rather than the pain of punishment that motivates people.

Maxim #431: Anonymous

It is when we forget ourselves that we do things which will be remembered.

Maxim #432: Anonymous

It is wise to keep in mind that no success or failure is necessarily final.

Maxim #433: Anonymous

It isn't the mountains ahead that wear you out, it's the grain of sand in your shoe.

Maxim #434: Anonymous

It isn't what you know but the simple things you don't overlook.

Maxim #435: Anonymous

It may be that your whole purpose in life is simply to serve as a warning to others.

Maxim #436: Anonymous

It speaks volumes for a person that when placed in quite different situations, they display the same spirit of moderation.

Maxim #437: Anonymous

It takes both a weapon, and two people, to commit a murder.

Maxim #438: Anonymous

It takes courage to know when you ought to be afraid.

Maxim #439: Anonymous

It's a sad state that government today supports and encourages a lifetime of "lazy poverty" at the expense of the rest of us.

Maxim #440: Anonymous

It's clever, but is it art?

Maxim #441: Anonymous

It's not what you know, it's how fast you can find it.

Maxim #442: Anonymous

It's only the view from where you sit that makes you feel defeat. Life is full of many aisles, so why don't you change your seat?

Maxim #443: Anonymous

It's smart to pick your friends - but not to pieces.

Maxim #444: Anonymous

Its quite true there's a fool born every minute. It's also quite true they don't die that fast.

Maxim #445: Anonymous

It's never about skin colour, always about culture and upbringing.

Maxim #446: Anonymous

Jone's Motto: Friends come and go, but enemies accumulate.

Maxim #447: Anonymous

Keep on sowing your seed, for you never know which will grow - perhaps it all will.

Maxim #448: Anonymous

Kill 'em with kindness: no one's tried THAT yet!

Maxim #449: Anonymous

Kindness is never out of fashion.

Maxim #450: Anonymous

Kindness is that perfume which cannot be poured
on others without getting a few drops on one's self.

Maxim #451: Anonymous

Knowing trees, I understand the meaning of
patience. Knowing grass. I can appreciate
persistence.

Maxim #452: Anonymous

Knowledge becomes wisdom only after it has been
put to practical use.

Maxim #453: Anonymous

Knowledge fills a large brain; it merely inflates a small one.

Maxim #454: Anonymous

LOVE, the feeling, is the fruit of LOVE, the verb.

Maxim #455: Anonymous

Lay up your treasures in heaven where there is no depreciation.

Maxim #456: Anonymous

Leaders are like eagles, they don't flock together; you find them one at a time.

Maxim #457: Anonymous

Leaders who aid others in growing are certain to experience growth in themselves.

Maxim #458: Anonymous

Leadership is about managing grown-ups, not raising children.

Maxim #459: Anonymous

Leadership, at its highest, consists of getting people to work for you when they are under no obligation to do so.

Maxim #460: Anonymous

Learn from yesterday, live for today, hope for tomorrow.

Maxim #461: Anonymous

Learn to follow counsel, serve faithfully, and magnify your calling, for God's kingdom is a kingdom of order.

Maxim #462: Anonymous

Learned men are the cisterns of knowledge, not the fountainheads.

Maxim #463: Anonymous

Learning is like rowing upstream. Advance or lose all.

Maxim #464: Anonymous

Leftists know they're wrong. That's why freedoms flowing from Right to Left never flow in the opposite direction.

Maxim #465: Anonymous

Let experience be your teacher, let challenges be the test of life.

Maxim #466: Anonymous

Let us not be desirous of vain glory, provoking one another, envying one another.

Maxim #467: Anonymous

Let your kids grow up without traditional role models and they will grow up pretty queer.

Maxim #468: Anonymous

Lewis's Law of Travel: The first piece of luggage out of the chute doesn't belong to anyone, ever.

Maxim #469: Anonymous

Liar's Law: First draw your curves - then plot your data.

Maxim #470: Anonymous

Liberals are not a part of the problem - they're the entire problem.

Maxim #471: Anonymous

Liberty is always unfinished business.

Maxim #472: Anonymous

Liberty is the right to choose, freedom is the result of that choice.

Maxim #473: Anonymous

Life is complex: it has a real part and an imaginary part.

Maxim #474: Anonymous

Life is hard by the yard, but by the inch, life's a cinch.

Maxim #475: Anonymous

Life is like quotations. Sometimes, it makes you laugh. Sometimes, it makes you cry. Most of the time, you don't get it.

Maxim #476: Anonymous

Life is there for the taking - or the refusing.

Maxim #477: Anonymous

Life may not be the party we hoped for, but while we're here we should dance.

Maxim #478: Anonymous

Life not only begins at forty - it begins to show.

Maxim #479: Anonymous

Listen to people twice as much as you speak.

Maxim #480: Anonymous

Little progress can be made merely by repressing what is bad. Our great hope lies in developing what is good.

Maxim #481: Anonymous

Living your life is a task so difficult, it has never been attempted before.

Maxim #482: Anonymous

Lockwood's Long Shot: The chances of getting eaten up by a lion on Main Street aren't one in a million, but once would be enough.

Maxim #483: Anonymous

Look at governmental programs for the past fifty years. Every single one - except for warfare - achieved the exact opposite of its announced goal.

Maxim #484: Anonymous

Look before you leap, for snakes among sweet flowers do creep.

Maxim #485: Anonymous

Love at first sight is one of the greatest labor-saving devices the world has ever seen.

Maxim #486: Anonymous

Love is for fools wise enough to take a chance.

Maxim #487: Anonymous

Love is in the offing. Be affectionate to one who adores you.

Maxim #488: Anonymous

Love is like a poisonous mushroom - you don't know if it is the real thing until it is too late.

Maxim #489: Anonymous

Love may conquer all, but it needs time as its field a general.

Maxim #490: Anonymous

Love will find a way. Indifference will find an excuse.

Maxim #491: Anonymous

Love your enemies: they'll go crazy trying to figure out what you're up to.

Maxim #492: Anonymous

M.D. to patient: First the good news - you're going to have a disease named after you.

Maxim #493: Anonymous

Maintain peace with men, war with their vices.

Maxim #494: Anonymous

Make new friends, but keep the old; those are silver, these are gold. Friendships that have stood the test, time and change are surely best.

Maxim #495: Anonymous

Make no judgments where you have no compassion.

Maxim #496: Anonymous

Make the mistakes of yesterday your lessons for today.

Maxim #497: Anonymous

Man must accept responsibility for himself ... There is no meaning to life except the meaning man gives his life by the unfolding of his powers.

Maxim #498: Anonymous

Man thrives only in the presence of a challenging environment.

Maxim #499: Anonymous

Manners are happy ways of doing things.

Maxim #500: Anonymous

Many a man gets to the top of the ladder, and then finds out it has been leaning against the wrong wall.

Maxim #501: Anonymous

Many a man would rather you heard his story than granted his request.

Maxim #502: Anonymous

Many bad artists will tell you that art is life. There's a subtle difference however. You can turn your back on art.

Maxim #503: Anonymous

Many great ideas have been lost because the people who had them could not stand being laughed at.

Maxim #504: Anonymous

Marital Freedom: The liberty that allows a husband to do exactly that which his wife pleases.

Maxim #505: Anonymous

Maugham's advice: Death is a very dull, dreary affair, and my advice to you is to have nothing whatsoever to do with it.

Maxim #506: Anonymous

Maybe you can't buy happiness, but these days you can certainly charge it.

Maxim #507: Anonymous

Meader's Law: Whatever happens to you, it will previously have happened to everyone you know, only more so.

Maxim #508: Anonymous

Meekness is great power under complete control.

Maxim #509: Anonymous

Memory builds a pathway that goes winding through the heart, and keeps friends close together, even though they are far apart.

Maxim #510: Anonymous

Men fight for freedom; then they begin to accumulate laws to take it away from them.

Maxim #511: Anonymous

Men have a tendency to believe what they least understand.

Maxim #512: Anonymous

Men never remember, but women never forget.

Maxim #513: Anonymous

Men still remember the first kiss after women have forgotten the last.

Maxim #514: Anonymous

Micro Credo: Never trust a computer bigger than you can lift.

Maxim #515: Anonymous

Miksch's Law: If a string has one end, then it has another end.

Maxim #516: Anonymous

Millihelen, adj: The amount of beauty required to launch one ship.

Maxim #517: Anonymous

Millions are idle, but it's comforting to know that most of them have jobs.

Maxim #518: Anonymous

Minors in Kansas City, Missouri, are not allowed to purchase cap pistols; they may buy shotguns freely, however.

Maxim #519: Anonymous

Mistakes are a great educator when one is honest enough to admit them and willing to learn from them.

Maxim #520: Anonymous

Mitchell's Law of Committees: Any simple problem can be made insoluble if enough meetings are held to discuss it.

Maxim #521: Anonymous

Money can't buy happiness, but it does quiet the nerves.

Maxim #522: Anonymous

Money cannot buy love, nor even friendship.

Maxim #523: Anonymous

Money doesn't always bring happiness. A man with ten million dollars is no happier than a man with nine million dollars.

Maxim #524: Anonymous

Money is a powerful aphrodisiac. But flowers work almost as well.

Maxim #525: Anonymous

Money will not buy happiness, but it will let you be unhappy in nice places.

Maxim #526: Anonymous

More powerful than the will to win is the courage to begin.

Maxim #527: Anonymous

Most of the mistakes of our life come from feeling when we ought to think and thinking when we ought to feel.

Maxim #528: Anonymous

Most of us will never do great things, but we can do small things in a great way.

Maxim #529: Anonymous

Most people are in favor of progress, it's the changes they don't like.

Maxim #530: Anonymous

Most writers regard the truth as their most valuable possession, and therefore are most economical in its use.

Maxim #531: Anonymous

Moveor Immotus. - "Motionless I am moved.".

Maxim #532: Anonymous

Much happiness is overlooked because it doesn't cost anything.

Maxim #533: Anonymous

My conscience doesn't keep me from doing things. It does keep me from enjoying them.

Maxim #534: Anonymous

My friend, why have you drifted so far away? All motion is relative, maybe it is you who have moved away by standing still.

Maxim #535: Anonymous

My how time flies when you're having fun!

Maxim #536: Anonymous

My job is never work -- the only time it seems like work is when I'd rather be doing something else.

Maxim #537: Anonymous

My opinions may have changed, but not the fact that I am right.

Maxim #538: Anonymous

My play was a complete success. The audience was a failure.

Maxim #539: Anonymous

My weight is perfect for my height - which varies.

Maxim #540: Anonymous

Natural laws have no pity.

Maxim #541: Anonymous

Necessity is the mother of invention.

Maxim #542: Anonymous

Neither sound nor thoughts can travel through a vacuum.

Maxim #543: Anonymous

Never argue with a fool - people might not know the difference.

Maxim #544: Anonymous

Never ascribe to malice that which can be adequately explained by ignorance.

Maxim #545: Anonymous

Never ask a question unless the answer makes a difference.

Maxim #546: Anonymous

Never build your emotional life on the weaknesses of others.

Maxim #547: Anonymous

Never commit yourself! Let someone else commit you.

Maxim #548: Anonymous

Never desert a comrade in need, in danger, or in trouble.

Maxim #549: Anonymous

Never give advice ... A wise man won't need it. A fool won't heed it.

Maxim #550: Anonymous

Never let a computer know you're in a hurry.

Maxim #551: Anonymous

Never let your schooling interfere with your education.

Maxim #552: Anonymous

Never put off until tomorrow what you can do today. There might be a law against it by that time.

Maxim #553: Anonymous

Never rise to speak until you have something to say, and when you have said it, cease.

Maxim #554: Anonymous

Never say goodbye, say farewell.

Maxim #555: Anonymous

Never say you know a man until you have divided an inheritance with him.

Maxim #556: Anonymous

Never try to guess your wife's size. Just buy her anything marked 'petite' and hold on to the receipt.

Maxim #557: Anonymous

New York is real. The rest is done with mirrors.

Maxim #558: Anonymous

Next to the prosperity of a good person, I am best pleased with the confusion of a rascal.

Maxim #559: Anonymous

Ninety percent of the things we tend to WORRY about we have no control over, so why worry about them?

Maxim #560: Anonymous

No decent career was ever founded on a public.

Maxim #561: Anonymous

No dream comes true until you wake up and go to work.

Maxim #562: Anonymous

No individual raindrop ever considers itself responsible for the flood.

Maxim #563: Anonymous

No man can ever be greater than his loftiest thoughts.

Maxim #564: Anonymous

No man was ever shot by his wife while doing the dishes.

Maxim #565: Anonymous

No man's life, liberty, or property are safe while the legislature is in session.

Maxim #566: Anonymous

No matter how much you do, you'll never do enough.

Maxim #567: Anonymous

No matter what occurs, there is always someone who believed it happened according to his pet theory.

Maxim #568: Anonymous

No one can enjoy freedom unless he is willing to surrender some part of it.

Maxim #569: Anonymous

No one knows his own servants as badly as the master.

Maxim #570: Anonymous

No one remembers learning how to use a spoon, it is something that is learned and not taught.

Maxim #571: Anonymous

No one who achieves success does so without acknowledging the help of others. The wise and confident acknowledge this help with gratitude.

Maxim #572: Anonymous

No person is either as happy or as unhappy as they imagine. Things are never as good or as bad as they seem.

Maxim #573: Anonymous

No poet sings because he must sing. At least no great poet does. A great poet sings because he chooses to sing.

Maxim #574: Anonymous

No problem is so formidable that you can't just walk away from it.

Maxim #575: Anonymous

No revenge is so heroic than that which torments envy by doing good.

Maxim #576: Anonymous

Nobody knows the age of the human race, but everybody agrees that it is old enough to know better.

Maxim #577: Anonymous

Nobody said computers were going to be polite.

Maxim #578: Anonymous

Nobody wants constructive criticism. It's all we can do to put up with constructive praise.

Maxim #579: Anonymous

None of us are responsible for all the things that happen to us, but we are responsible for the way we act when they do happen.

Maxim #580: Anonymous

Not in our future, yet in the past! Premarital choices, to make love - last!

Maxim #581: Anonymous

Not to live through, but to live up to.

Maxim #582: Anonymous

Nothing in excess.

Maxim #583: Anonymous

Nothing in this world is impossible to a willing heart.

Maxim #584: Anonymous

Nothing marks the character of a young man more than failure.

Maxim #585: Anonymous

Nothing of importance is ever done without a plan.

Maxim #586: Anonymous

Nothing ventured, nothing gained.

Maxim #587: Anonymous

Nothing would be done at all, if a man waited 'til he could do so well that no one could find fault with it.

Maxim #588: Anonymous

Now and then an innocent man is sent to the legislature.

Maxim #589: Anonymous

Obedience without faith is possible, but not faith without obedience.

Maxim #590: Anonymous

Offering kindness to a barbarian never changed it's religion.

Maxim #591: Anonymous

Often I think writing is a sheer paring away of oneself leaving always something thinner, barer, more meager.

Maxim #592: Anonymous

Often statistics are used as a drunken man uses lampposts - for support rather than illumination.

Maxim #593: Anonymous

Ogden's Law: The sooner you fall behind, the more time you have to catch up.

Maxim #594: Anonymous

Old MacDonald had an agricultural real estate tax abatement.

Maxim #595: Anonymous

Old age may seem a long way off. But on the day it doesn't, it will be too late to do anything about it.

Maxim #596: Anonymous

Old keys do not unlock new doors.

Maxim #597: Anonymous

On-line, adj.: The idea that a human being should always be accessible to a computer.

Maxim #598: Anonymous

Once upon a time only Washington's face was on our money, now Washington's hands are on it too.

Maxim #599: Anonymous

Once you have learned to love, You will have learned to live.

Maxim #600: Anonymous

One ABC of Christianity: 'Always Be Cheerful' [1 Thessalonians 5:16]

Maxim #601: Anonymous

One can easily judge the character of a person by the way they treat people who can do nothing for them.

Maxim #602: Anonymous

One disadvantage of having nothing to do is you can't stop and rest.

Maxim #603: Anonymous

One doesn't get chances - one takes chances.

Maxim #604: Anonymous

One dog barks at something, a hundred bark at the sound.

Maxim #605: Anonymous

One fact is better than one hundred apologies.

Maxim #606: Anonymous

One man tells a falsehood, a hundred repeat it as true.

Maxim #607: Anonymous

One moment of patience may ward off a great disaster; one moment of impatience may ruin a whole life.

Maxim #608: Anonymous

One nice thing about egotists: they don't talk about other people.

Maxim #609: Anonymous

One of society's biggest problems today is that we've allowed relationships to be accepted as impermanent, particularly marriage.

Maxim #610: Anonymous

One of the horrors of hell is the undying memory of a misspent life.

Maxim #611: Anonymous

One should be more concerned about what his conscience whispers than about what other people shout.

Maxim #612: Anonymous

One who lacks courage to start has already finished

Maxim #613: Anonymous

Only one can keep a secret.

Maxim #614: Anonymous

Only the incompetent and mediocre are always at their best.

Maxim #615: Anonymous

Opportunities always look bigger going than coming.

Maxim #616: Anonymous

Opportunities are often missed because we are broadcasting when we should be listening.

Maxim #617: Anonymous

Opportunity is ever worth expecting; let your hook be ever hanging ready, the fish will be in the pool where you least imagine it to be.

Maxim #618: Anonymous

Oregon, n.: Eighty billion gallons of water with no place to go on Saturday night.

Maxim #619: Anonymous

Others will follow your footsteps easier than they will your advice.

Maxim #620: Anonymous

Our clock of life, wound up in the womb, begins to run down at the very moment of birth. Everyday, we die a little.

Maxim #621: Anonymous

Our favorite attitude should be gratitude

Maxim #622: Anonymous

Our five senses are incomplete without the sixth --
a sense of humor.

Maxim #623: Anonymous

Our health always seems much more valuable after
we lose it.

Maxim #624: Anonymous

Our hopes are but memories reversed.

Maxim #625: Anonymous

Our prejudices are our robbers, they rob us valuable things in life.

Maxim #626: Anonymous

Our thanks to God should always precede our requests.

Maxim #627: Anonymous

Pain is inevitable. Suffering is optional.

Maxim #628: Anonymous

Parkinson's First Law: Work expands so as to fill the time available for its completion.

Maxim #629: Anonymous

Past failures are guideposts to success.

Maxim #630: Anonymous

Past performance produces present privileges.

Maxim #631: Anonymous

Patience and perseverance surmount every difficulty.

Maxim #632: Anonymous

Peace won by the compromise of principles is a short-lived achievement.

Maxim #633: Anonymous

People are attracted to happy people.

Maxim #634: Anonymous

People are more violently opposed to fur than leather because it's safer to harass rich women than motorcycle gangs.

Maxim #635: Anonymous

People fail many times, but they become failures only when they begin to blame someone else.

Maxim #636: Anonymous

People have a way of becoming what you encourage them to be, not what you nag them to be.

Maxim #637: Anonymous

People have to pretend you're a bad person so they don't feel guilty about the things they did to you.

Maxim #638: Anonymous

People should know what you stand for. They should also know what you won't stand for.

Maxim #639: Anonymous

People sitting on top of the world, usually arrived there standing up.

Maxim #640: Anonymous

People who do things that count, never stop to count them.

Maxim #641: Anonymous

People who fall for everything always stand for nothing.

Maxim #642: Anonymous

People who have no faith in themselves seldom have faith in others.

Maxim #643: Anonymous

People who like others are people others like.

Maxim #644: Anonymous

People who run down others are taking a roundabout way of praising themselves.

> **Maxim #645: Anonymous**
>
> People who say it cannot be done should not interrupt those who are doing it.

> **Maxim #646: Anonymous**
>
> People will be happy in about the same degree that they are helpful.

> **Maxim #647: Anonymous**
>
> People will buy anything that's one to a customer.

> **Maxim #648: Anonymous**
>
> People will do tomorrow what they did today because that is what they did yesterday.

Maxim #649: Anonymous

People will laugh at you, but let not that prevent you.

Maxim #650: Anonymous

Pick the right person the first time. The headaches you save will be your own.

Maxim #651: Anonymous

Pity Poor Pandora's Premarital Promiscuities ... Presently, Permanently, Propagating Perplexing Planetary People Problems!

Maxim #652: Anonymous

Plan well before you take the journey. Remember the carpenter's rule: Measure twice, cut once.

Maxim #653: Anonymous

Plan your work. Work your plan.

Maxim #654: Anonymous

Plow deep while sluggards sleep.

Maxim #655: Anonymous

Pohl's law: Nothing is so good that somebody, somewhere, will not hate it.

Maxim #656: Anonymous

Politicians are like diapers. They both need changing regularly and for the same reason.

Maxim #657: Anonymous

Politicians should never put themselves first: governments should put people first and all of us should put our country first.

Maxim #658: Anonymous

Politics isn't too bad a profession. If you succeed, there are many rewards. If you disgrace yourself, you can always write a book.

Maxim #659: Anonymous

Poster in Belgrade tourist office: Visit the Soviet Union before it visits you.

Maxim #660: Anonymous

Pound for pound, the amoeba is the most vicious animal on earth.

Maxim #661: Anonymous

Practice random kindness and senseless acts of beauty.

Maxim #662: Anonymous

Prayer is a passport to heaven. Your communication with God.

Maxim #663: Anonymous

Prayer moves the hand that moves the universe.

Maxim #664: Anonymous

Prejudice is a great timesaver. It enables you to form opinions without bothering to get facts.

Maxim #665: Anonymous

Prejudice is being down on something you're not up on.

Maxim #666: Anonymous

Premarital Promiscuities Presently Propagating Perplexing People Problems

Maxim #667: Anonymous

Preserve the old, but know the new.

Maxim #668: Anonymous

Privacy is essential to Liberty.

Maxim #669: Anonymous

Private bravery is often the price of personal victory.

Maxim #670: Anonymous

Professionalism: It's NOT the job you DO, It's HOW you DO the job.

Maxim #671: Anonymous

Profits are an opinion, cash is a fact.

Maxim #672: Anonymous

Promise only what you can deliver. Then deliver more than you promise.

Maxim #673: Anonymous

Promptness is its own reward, if one lives by the clock instead of the sword.

Maxim #674: Anonymous

Pros are people who do jobs well even when they don't feel like it.

Maxim #675: Anonymous

Put people on hold when possible.

Maxim #676: Anonymous

Quidquid latine dictum sit, altum viditur. (Whatever is said in Latin sounds profound.)

Maxim #677: Anonymous

Quigley's Law: Whoever has any authority over you, no matter how small, will attempt to use it.

Maxim #678: Anonymous

RELIABLE: Sometimes capable of giving the same results.

Maxim #679: Anonymous

Rather suffer an injustice than commit one.

Maxim #680: Anonymous

Reading is thinking with someone else's head instead of one's own.

Maxim #681: Anonymous

Real brothers and sisters obey our Father's laws.
Others cast out - even from heaven itself.

Maxim #682: Anonymous

Real courage is when you know you're licked before
you begin, but you begin anyway and see it
through no matter what.

Maxim #683: Anonymous

Real leaders are ordinary people with extraordinary
determination.

Maxim #684: Anonymous

Reality is an illusion caused by lack of alcohol.

Maxim #685: Anonymous

Reality is an obstacle to hallucination.

Maxim #686: Anonymous

Regarding trade relations, most people would like to.

Maxim #687: Anonymous

Religion is like holding on to a rock in the middle of a raging river; faith is learning how to swim.

Maxim #688: Anonymous

Remember that great love and great achievements involve great risk.

Maxim #689: Anonymous

Remember that the faith that moves mountains always carries a pick.

Maxim #690: Anonymous

Remember that your failures are the seeds of your most glorious successes. Be sad if you must, but don't despair.

Maxim #691: Anonymous

Remember the turtle -- He never makes any progress till he sticks his neck out.

Maxim #692: Anonymous

Remember, drive defensively! And of course, the best defense is a good offense!

Maxim #693: Anonymous

Remember, people will judge you by your actions, not your intentions. You may have a heart of gold - but so does a hard-boiled egg.

Maxim #694: Anonymous

Remember, we all stumble, every one of us.

Maxim #695: Anonymous

Remember: LSD absorbs 47 times it own weight in excess reality.

Maxim #696: Anonymous

Remember: the average is as close to the bottom as it is to the top.

Maxim #697: Anonymous

Republicans usually wear hats and clean their paint brushes.

Maxim #698: Anonymous

Reputation is the shell a man discards when he leaves life for immortality. His character he takes with him.

Maxim #699: Anonymous

Revenue is vanity... margin is sanity... cash is king.

Maxim #700: Anonymous

Running into debt isn't so bad. It's running into creditors that hurts.

Maxim #701: Anonymous

Say's Law: Supply creates its own demand.

Maxim #702: Anonymous

Secular education can make men clever, but it cannot make them good.

Maxim #703: Anonymous

Seeing yourself as you want to be is the key to personal growth.

Maxim #704: Anonymous

Seek joy in what you give not in what you get.

Maxim #705: Anonymous

Seek the friend who's hand helped you and tell them what they mean to you.

Maxim #706: Anonymous

Self-determination is fine but needs to be tempered with self-control.

Maxim #707: Anonymous

Self-praise is no recommendation.

Maxim #708: Anonymous

Set Your Goals High Enough To Inspire You And Low Enough To Encourage You.

Maxim #709: Anonymous

Seven days without prayer makes one weak.

Maxim #710: Anonymous

Shared joy is joy doubled. Shared sorrow is sorrow halved.

Maxim #711: Anonymous

Shaw's Principle: Build a system that even a fool can use, and only a fool will want to use it.

Maxim #712: Anonymous

She's learned to say things with her eyes that others waste time putting into words.

Maxim #713: Anonymous

Shocked to hear one student turn to curse another "May Hamas abduct your mother, eat your baby, and sell your organs to the Chinese."

Maxim #714: Anonymous

Sign in a cluttered, old-fashioned hardware store: "We've got it, if we can find it."

Maxim #715: Anonymous

Silicon Valley is a graveyard. Failure is Silicon Valley's greatest strength.

Maxim #716: Anonymous

So far the only successful substitute for brains is silence.

Maxim #717: Anonymous

Solitude is the despair of fools, the torment of the wicked, and the joy of the good.

Maxim #718: Anonymous

Solving the problem does not pay as well as creating another.

Maxim #719: Anonymous

Some lies are so well disguised to resemble truth, that we should be poor judges of the truth not to believe them.

Maxim #720: Anonymous

Some people forget to plant in the spring, idle away the summer hours and then expect to reap in the fall.

Maxim #721: Anonymous

Some people grin and bear it; others smile and do it.

Maxim #722: Anonymous

Some people study all their life, and at death they have learned everything except how to think.

Maxim #723: Anonymous

Someone has compared California to a granola cereal; when you take away the fruits and the nuts, all you have left are the flakes.

Maxim #724: Anonymous

Sometimes I wish I were a little kid again, skinned knees are easier to fix than broken hearts.

Maxim #725: Anonymous

Sometimes the best way to figure out who you are is to get to that place where you don't have to be anything else.

Maxim #726: Anonymous

Sometimes the crowd is right.

Maxim #727: Anonymous

Somewhere, something incredible is waiting to be known.

Maxim #728: Anonymous

Start with what is right rather than what is acceptable.

Maxim #729: Anonymous

Stop day dreaming about success. Go out and obtain it.

Maxim #730: Anonymous

Study reveals that 5 out of 4 Americans have trouble with fractions.

Maxim #731: Anonymous

Stult's Report: Our problems are mostly behind us. What we have to do now is fight the solutions.

Maxim #732: Anonymous

Subtlety is the art of saying what you think and getting out of the way before it is understood.

Maxim #733: Anonymous

Success comes in cans, failure in cant's.

Maxim #734: Anonymous

Success does not come to those who wait ... and it does not wait for anyone to come to it.

Maxim #735: Anonymous

Success goes to your head, failure to your heart.

Maxim #736: Anonymous

Success in management - at any level - depends on the ability to pick the right people for the right jobs.

Maxim #737: Anonymous

Success is just a matter of luck, all you need to do is ask a failure. History may be written by academics but it's rarely created by them.

Maxim #738: Anonymous

Success is more dependent on the backbone than the wishbone.

Maxim #739: Anonymous

Success is still the constant application of the Golden Rule.

Maxim #740: Anonymous

Success is the proper utilization of failure.

> **Maxim #741: Anonymous**
>
> Successful leaders have the courage to take action where others hesitate.

> **Maxim #742: Anonymous**
>
> Such torment when hypocrites blame - each against themselves!

> **Maxim #743: Anonymous**
>
> Suffering fools gladly creates far too many glad fools.

> **Maxim #744: Anonymous**
>
> Sure, he's a bum. But even a bum has feelings.

Maxim #745: Anonymous

Swallowing your pride seldom leads to indigestion.

Maxim #746: Anonymous

Take charge of your attitude. Don't let someone else choose it for you.

Maxim #747: Anonymous

Take pride in how far you have come, have faith in how far you can go.

Maxim #748: Anonymous

Taking the line of least resistance still makes both men and rivers crooked.

Maxim #749: Anonymous

Taxes are going up so fast, the government is likely to price itself out of the market.

Maxim #750: Anonymous

Taxes are not levied for the benefit of the taxed.

Maxim #751: Anonymous

Technology does not drive change -- it enables change.

Maxim #752: Anonymous

Tell the boss what you really think of him ... and the truth shall set you free.

Maxim #753: Anonymous

Temptation usually comes in through a door that has deliberately been left open.

Maxim #754: Anonymous

That which we obtain too easily, we esteem too lightly.

Maxim #755: Anonymous

The 500 most commonly used words have an average of 28 meanings each.

Maxim #756: Anonymous

The Kennedy Constant: Don't get mad-get even.

Maxim #757: Anonymous

The Ten Commandments are not multiple choice

Maxim #758: Anonymous

The average man's opinions are generally of more value to himself than to anyone else.

Maxim #759: Anonymous

The best angle from which to approach a problem is the Try-angle.

Maxim #760: Anonymous

The best answer to answer to anger is silence.

Maxim #761: Anonymous

The best defense against logic is ignorance.

Maxim #762: Anonymous

The best investment you can make is hard work.

Maxim #763: Anonymous

The best teacher is the person who gets others to teach. We learn when we teach.

Maxim #764: Anonymous

The best throw of the dice is to throw them away.

> ### Maxim #765: Anonymous
> The best vitamin for making friends, B-1.

> ### Maxim #766: Anonymous
> The best way to appreciate your job is to imagine yourself without one.

> ### Maxim #767: Anonymous
> The best way to get and keep good people is to give them room to grow.

> ### Maxim #768: Anonymous
> The best way to keep good intentions from dying is to execute them.

Maxim #769: Anonymous

The best way to knock the chip off your neighbor's shoulder is to pat him on the back.

Maxim #770: Anonymous

The best way to succeed in life is to act on the advice we give to others.

Maxim #771: Anonymous

The biggest step you can take is the one you take when you meet the other person halfway.

Maxim #772: Anonymous

The bird chooses the tree, not the tree the bird.

Maxim #773: Anonymous

The bland leadeth the bland and they both shall fall into the kitsch.

Maxim #774: Anonymous

The boundaries of a man's mind are set by himself, and no one else.

Maxim #775: Anonymous

The broad general rule is that a man is about as big as the things that make him angry.

Maxim #776: Anonymous

The chief enemy of good is better.

Maxim #777: Anonymous

The compromise will always be more expensive than either of the suggestions it is compromising.

Maxim #778: Anonymous

The creme will rise to the top regardless of ethnicities.

Maxim #779: Anonymous

The customer is the final inspector.

Maxim #780: Anonymous

The cynic who doesn't believe in anything still wants you to believe him.

Maxim #781: Anonymous

The days just prior to marriage are like a snappy introduction to a tedious book.

Maxim #782: Anonymous

The difference between goals and mission is reflected in the difference between I want to get married and I want to have a successful marriage.

Maxim #783: Anonymous

The difference between perseverance and obstinacy is that one often comes from a strong will, and the other from a strong won't.

Maxim #784: Anonymous

The difficulties we experience Always illuminate the lessons we need most.

Maxim #785: Anonymous

The distance you have to park from your apartment increases in proportion to the weight of the packages you are carrying.

Maxim #786: Anonymous

The dogs bark but the caravan moves on.

Maxim #787: Anonymous

The earth is like a tiny grain of sand, only much, much heavier.

Maxim #788: Anonymous

The essence of intelligence is skill in extracting meaning from everyday experience.

> ### Maxim #789: Anonymous
>
> The essence of life is taking over.

> ### Maxim #790: Anonymous
>
> The explanation requiring the fewest assumptions is the most likely to be correct.

> ### Maxim #791: Anonymous
>
> The finest eloquence is that which gets things done.

> ### Maxim #792: Anonymous
>
> The first 90 percent of the task takes 90 percent of the time, the last 10 percent takes the other 90 percent.

Maxim #793: Anonymous

The first draught a man drinks ought to be for thirst, the second for nourishment, the third for pleasure, the fourth for madness.

Maxim #794: Anonymous

The first impression one gets of a new ruler and his brains is from seeing the men he has chosen to have around him.

Maxim #795: Anonymous

The first step of handling anything is gaining an ability to face it.

Maxim #796: Anonymous

The first thing I do in the morning is brush my teeth and sharpen my tongue.

Maxim #797: Anonymous

The future belongs to those who dare.

Maxim #798: Anonymous

The future lies before you, like paths of pure white snow. Be careful how you tread it, for every step will show.

Maxim #799: Anonymous

The goal of science is to build better mousetraps. The goal of nature is to build better mice.

Maxim #800: Anonymous

The good thing about being young is that you are not experienced enough to know you cannot possibly do the things you are doing.

Maxim #801: Anonymous

The happiness in this life does not consist of being devoid of passion, but mastering them.

Maxim #802: Anonymous

The harder you fall, the higher you bounce.

Maxim #803: Anonymous

The heart is wiser than the intellect.

Maxim #804: Anonymous

The higher you go the more dependent you become on others.

Maxim #805: Anonymous

The highest function of the teacher consists not so much in imparting knowledge as in stimulating the pupil in its love and pursuit.

Maxim #806: Anonymous

The history of the world is the record of man in quest of his daily bread and butter.

Maxim #807: Anonymous

The key to getting everything you want is to never put all your begs in one ask-it!

Maxim #808: Anonymous

The key to happiness is having dreams. The key to success is making your dreams come true.

Maxim #809: Anonymous

The key to understanding others is to first understand yourself

Maxim #810: Anonymous

The kind of ancestors we have had is not as important as the kind of descendants our ancestors have.

Maxim #811: Anonymous

The largest barrier to success is removing the mattress from one's back in the morning.

Maxim #812: Anonymous

The less people know about how sausages and laws are made, the better they'll sleep at night.

Maxim #813: Anonymous

The less you know about an opportunity, the more attractive it is.

Maxim #814: Anonymous

The light & inspiration of men is temporary. The light & inspiration of God is always.

Maxim #815: Anonymous

The light that burns twice as bright, burns half as long.

Maxim #816: Anonymous

The love required to "stay together for the sake of the children" replaced by the hate required to destroy all for the sake of a pronoun.

Maxim #817: Anonymous

The major justification for a life is the happiness and reward it brings to other lives.

Maxim #818: Anonymous

The majority of your governmental organizations do not exist to solve problems but to create problems that they might exist.

Maxim #819: Anonymous

The man is free to rule his world, not his world rule him.

Maxim #820: Anonymous

The man who appeals to the best side of his fellows is rarely disappointed.

Maxim #821: Anonymous

The man who really wants to do something finds a way, the other finds an excuse.

Maxim #822: Anonymous

The manner in which it is given is often worth more than the gift.

Maxim #823: Anonymous

The master's eye makes the horse fat.

Maxim #824: Anonymous

The measure of a truly great man is the courtesy with which he treats lesser men.

Maxim #825: Anonymous

The mistake to not question their sacred cow is to prefer to clean up after it. Ever worse the herd.

Maxim #826: Anonymous

The moon is a planet just like the Earth, only it is even deader.

Maxim #827: Anonymous

The more adapted you are, the less adaptable you tend to be.

Maxim #828: Anonymous

The more we disagree, the more chance there is that at least one of us is right.

Maxim #829: Anonymous

The more you do of what you've done, the more you'll have of what you've got.

Maxim #830: Anonymous

The more you know, the less you need to show.

Maxim #831: Anonymous

The most effective answer to an insult is silence.

Maxim #832: Anonymous

The new Congressmen say they're going to turn the government around. I hope I don't get run over again.

Maxim #833: Anonymous

The new organization is edgeless, permeable, amorphous... constantly re-forming according to need.

Maxim #834: Anonymous

The next dreadful thing to a battle lost is a battle won.

Maxim #835: Anonymous

The one thing you cannot teach a person is common sense.

Maxim #836: Anonymous

The only problem with being a man of leisure is that you can never stop and take a rest.

Maxim #837: Anonymous

The only reason I might go to the funeral is to make absolutely sure that he's dead.

Maxim #838: Anonymous

The only reason some people listen to reason is to gain time for rebuttal.

Maxim #839: Anonymous

The only thing necessary for the triumph of evil is for good men to do nothing.

Maxim #840: Anonymous

The only thing that hurts more than paying an income tax is not having to pay an income tax.

Maxim #841: Anonymous

The pioneer who fought for his liberties now has descendants who take them.

Maxim #842: Anonymous

The price of living is giving.

Maxim #843: Anonymous

The price of peace is righteousness.

Maxim #844: Anonymous

The problem with political jokes is that they get elected.

Maxim #845: Anonymous

The race is not always to the swift but to those who keep on running.

Maxim #846: Anonymous

The real danger is not that computers will begin to think like men, but that men will being to think like computers.

Maxim #847: Anonymous

The revolution will not be televised.

Maxim #848: Anonymous

The reward of a good deed is to have done it.

Maxim #849: Anonymous

The road to perfection is always under construction.

Maxim #850: Anonymous

The road to success is lined with many tempting parking spaces

Maxim #851: Anonymous

The search for the perfect venture can turn into procrastination. Your idea may or may not have merit. The key is to get started.

Maxim #852: Anonymous

The secret to happiness is not in doing what one likes to do, but in liking what one has to do.

Maxim #853: Anonymous

The shortest distance between new friends is a smile.

Maxim #854: Anonymous

The shortest distance between two people is laughter.

Maxim #855: Anonymous

The smallest good deed is better than the grandest intention.

Maxim #856: Anonymous

The staggering amount trees have before created, even earths volcanic past testifies that all emissions are digestable.

Maxim #857: Anonymous

The storm also beats on the house that is built on the rock.

Maxim #858: Anonymous

The subconscious mind is a mental fireless cooker where ideas simmer & develop.

Maxim #859: Anonymous

The supreme test of a person is his ability to make things go right.

Maxim #860: Anonymous

The three faithful things in life are money, a dog, and an old woman.

Maxim #861: Anonymous

The trick is to hold opinions without letting opinions hold you.

Maxim #862: Anonymous

The trouble with doing something right the first time is that nobody appreciates how difficult it was.

Maxim #863: Anonymous

The trouble with self-made men is that they tend to worship their creator.

Maxim #864: Anonymous

The trouble with the average family budget is that at the end of the money there's too much month left.

Maxim #865: Anonymous

The trouble with the average family today is that it's hard to support it and the government on one income.

Maxim #866: Anonymous

The two hardest things to handle in life are failure & success.

Maxim #867: Anonymous

The two most common things in the universe are hydrogen and stupidity.

Maxim #868: Anonymous

The universe does not have laws - it has habits, and habits can be broken.

Maxim #869: Anonymous

The universe rearranges itself to accommodate your picture of reality.

Maxim #870: Anonymous

The very act of believing creates strength of its own.

Maxim #871: Anonymous

The water we drink has to be purified, but look at the trash we feed our minds.

Maxim #872: Anonymous

The way to kill time profitably is to work it to death.

Maxim #873: Anonymous

The way to learn is to begin.

Maxim #874: Anonymous

The weed of crime bears bitter fruit.

Maxim #875: Anonymous

The well being of the people is the supreme law.

Maxim #876: Anonymous

The well-tended front lawn is the modern moat that keeps the barbarians -- other people-at bay.

Maxim #877: Anonymous

The wheel that squeaks the loudest is the first to be replaced.

Maxim #878: Anonymous

The words you speak today should be soft and tender... for tomorrow you may have to eat them.

Maxim #879: Anonymous

The work we do on ourselves becomes our gift to everyone else.

Maxim #880: Anonymous

The worst thing about a bore is not that he won't stop talking, but that he won't let you stop listening.

Maxim #881: Anonymous

Then went the Pharisees, and took counsel how they might entangle him in his talk.

Maxim #882: Anonymous

There are always two choices, two paths to take. One is easy. And its only reward is that it's easy.

Maxim #883: Anonymous

There are few people more often in the wrong than those who cannot endure to be thought so.

Maxim #884: Anonymous

There are hundreds of languages in the world but a smile speaks them all.

Maxim #885: Anonymous

There are more old drunkards than old doctors.

Maxim #886: Anonymous

There are no traffic jams in the second mile.

Maxim #887: Anonymous

There are no traffic jams when you go the extra mile.

Maxim #888: Anonymous

There are people so near nothing that they are everywhere without being seen.

Maxim #889: Anonymous

There are two kinds of people in the world -- those you love, and those you don't understand.

Maxim #890: Anonymous

There are two ways we can meet a difficulty: either we can alter the difficulty or we can alter ourselves to meet it.

Maxim #891: Anonymous

There are usually two sides to every argument, but never an end.

Maxim #892: Anonymous

There is a great discovery still to be made in Literature: that of paying literary men by the quantity they do NOT write.

> ### Maxim #893: Anonymous
>
> There is a tendency for the person in the most powerful position in an organization to spend all his time serving on committees and signing letters.

> ### Maxim #894: Anonymous
>
> There is always someone worse off than yourself.

> ### Maxim #895: Anonymous
>
> There is more to life that being entertained.

> ### Maxim #896: Anonymous
>
> There is no freedom without the power to defend it.

Maxim #897: Anonymous

There is no greater treasure than the respect and love of a true friend.

Maxim #898: Anonymous

There is no growth without discontent.

Maxim #899: Anonymous

There is no one from whom you cannot learn something: try it!

Maxim #900: Anonymous

There is no such thing as accidental failure. All failure is at least half imposed.

Maxim #901: Anonymous

There is no teaching force like a good man's life.

Maxim #902: Anonymous

There is nothing as cheap and weak in debate as assertion that is not backed by facts.

Maxim #903: Anonymous

There is nothing more destructive of physical and mental health than the isolation of you from me, of us from them.

Maxim #904: Anonymous

There is nothing wrong with making mistakes. Just don't respond with errors.

Maxim #905: Anonymous

There is one way to handle the ignorant and malicious critic. Ignore him.

Maxim #906: Anonymous

There was a generation gap between Lucifer and his Father, but another Son understood deeper principles and carried on his Father's work.

Maxim #907: Anonymous

There was an educational channel in the good old days; it was called 'off'.

Maxim #908: Anonymous

There's no room in the drug world for amateurs.

Maxim #909: Anonymous

There's no such thing as a dangerous weapon, only dangerous men.

Maxim #910: Anonymous

There's nothing wrong with having nothing to say unless you insist on saying it.

Maxim #911: Anonymous

There's times peoples just be tired of peoples.

Maxim #912: Anonymous

They also surf who only stand on waves.

Maxim #913: Anonymous

They say an elephant never forgets, but what's he got to remember?

Maxim #914: Anonymous

Think all you speak, but speak not all you think.

Maxim #915: Anonymous

Think highly of yourself, for the world takes you at your own estimate.

Maxim #916: Anonymous

Think of what others ought to be like, then start being like that yourself.

Maxim #917: Anonymous

Think twice before you speak, then say it to yourself first.

Maxim #918: Anonymous

Thinking is only a process of talking to yourself.

Maxim #919: Anonymous

Thinking things has been done through the ages; knowing things remains to be done.

Maxim #920: Anonymous

This is a good time to punt work.

Maxim #921: Anonymous

This is my rule of married life: it's better to be happy than to be right.

Maxim #922: Anonymous

This will be a memorable month - no matter how hard you try to forget it.

Maxim #923: Anonymous

Those that are silent profess consent.

Maxim #924: Anonymous

Those who are afraid of doing too much always do too little.

Maxim #925: Anonymous

Those who spiritualize tell spiritual lies, because they lack spiritual eyes.

Maxim #926: Anonymous

Time flies, but remember: you are the navigator.

Maxim #927: Anonymous

Time invested in improving ourselves cuts down on time wasted in disapproving of others.

Maxim #928: Anonymous

Time is nature's way of keeping everything from happening at once.

Maxim #929: Anonymous

Time spent in getting even would be better spent in getting ahead.

Maxim #930: Anonymous

To abuse wine is to abuse life itself.

Maxim #931: Anonymous

To be free it is not enough to beat the system, one must beat the system every day.

Maxim #932: Anonymous

To be free of destructive stress, don't sweat the small stuff, and this by realizing that all stuff is small.

Maxim #933: Anonymous

To be loved is to live forever in someone's heart.

Maxim #934: Anonymous

To be scared is sensible, to be comfortable is suicidal.

Maxim #935: Anonymous

To be what we are, and to become what we are capable of is the only end in life.

Maxim #936: Anonymous

To believe is to be strong. Doubt cramps energy. Belief is power.

Maxim #937: Anonymous

To do great, important tasks, two things are necessary: a plan and not quite enough time.

Maxim #938: Anonymous

To dream of the person you would like to be is to waste the person you are.

Maxim #939: Anonymous

To err is human and to blame it on a computer is even more so.

Maxim #940: Anonymous

To err is human, to blame the next guy even more so.

Maxim #941: Anonymous

To err may become inhuman.

Maxim #942: Anonymous

To feel 'fit as a fiddle' you must tone down your middle.

Maxim #943: Anonymous

To get something done, a committee should consist of no more than three men, two of them absent.

Maxim #944: Anonymous

To get to heaven, turn right and keep straight.

Maxim #945: Anonymous

To have the last word with a woman - apologize.

Maxim #946: Anonymous

To keep your friends treat them kindly; to kill them, treat them often.

Maxim #947: Anonymous

To obtain maximum attention, it's hard to beat a good, big mistake.

Maxim #948: Anonymous

To profit from good advice requires as much wisdom as to give it.

Maxim #949: Anonymous

To save oneself, one must take risks and struggle.

Maxim #950: Anonymous

To select the wrong person for a job is a common mistake; not to remove him / her is a fatal weakness.

Maxim #951: Anonymous

To stay young requires unceasing cultivation of the ability to unlearn old falsehoods.

Maxim #952: Anonymous

To write it, it took three months; to conceive it --three minutes; to collect the data on it -- all my life.

Maxim #953: Anonymous

Today is the first day of the rest of your life.

Maxim #954: Anonymous

Today's progress was yesterday's plan.

Maxim #955: Anonymous

Too many of us speak twice before we think.

Maxim #956: Anonymous

Torture the data long enough and they will confess to anything.

Maxim #957: Anonymous

Traveler, there is no path, paths are made by walking.

Maxim #958: Anonymous

True glory lies in noble deeds.

Maxim #959: Anonymous

True happiness comes from doing what's right not just doing what makes you feel good.

Maxim #960: Anonymous

True love is the outward demonstration of inward conviction.

Maxim #961: Anonymous

True prosperity is the result of well-placed confidence in ourselves and our fellow man.

Maxim #962: Anonymous

Trust can be a powerful weapon.

Maxim #963: Anonymous

Truth and tears clear the way to a deep and lasting friendship.

Maxim #964: Anonymous

Truth comes only to a prepared mind.

Maxim #965: Anonymous

Try to be the best of whatever you are, even if what you are is no good.

Maxim #966: Anonymous

Try to become the kind of person that people are anxious to see you as, and after you leave, they will have a lot of thinking to do.

Maxim #967: Anonymous

Turn your stumbling blocks into stepping stones.

Maxim #968: Anonymous

Two things rob people of their peace of mind : work unfinished and work not yet begun.

Maxim #969: Anonymous

Under capitalism man exploits man; under socialism the reverse is true.

Maxim #970: Anonymous

Use disappointments as material for patience.

Maxim #971: Anonymous

Value friendship for what there is in it, not for what can be gotten out of it.

Maxim #972: Anonymous

Virtues paraded hide vices; like those strong odors used to hide bad smells.

Maxim #973: Anonymous

Walking around urban war zones always consider carrying cast iron. The pan is mightier than the sword.

Maxim #974: Anonymous

Wasting time is an important part of life.

Maxim #975: Anonymous

We act the way we dress. Neglected and untidy clothes reflect a neglected and untidy mind.

Maxim #976: Anonymous

We all leave footprints in the sand, the question is, will we be a big heal, or a great soul.

Maxim #977: Anonymous

We are all friends at heart. We just need more tragedies to prove it to ourselves.

Maxim #978: Anonymous

We are changed as we change our environment.

Maxim #979: Anonymous

We are drowning in information and starved for knowledge.

Maxim #980: Anonymous

We are not primarily on this earth to see through one another, but to see one another through.

Maxim #981: Anonymous

We are not punished for our sins but by them.

Maxim #982: Anonymous

We are the people our parents warned us about.

Maxim #983: Anonymous

We came here to serve not be served.

Maxim #984: Anonymous

We can only paint with the colors we've stirred up within us.

Maxim #985: Anonymous

We cannot direct the wind but we can adjust the sails.

Maxim #986: Anonymous

We did not inherit the land from our forefathers- we are borrowing it from our children.

Maxim #987: Anonymous

We make a living by what we get; we make a life by what we give.

Maxim #988: Anonymous

We must be prepared to be part of the cure and not remain part of the problem.

> **Maxim #989: Anonymous**
>
> We mustn't let our passions destroy our dreams.

> **Maxim #990: Anonymous**
>
> We really don't have any enemies. It's just that some of our best friends are trying to kill us.

> **Maxim #991: Anonymous**
>
> We sought the mutant due for lynching, Not a trace was there to find. I told the others--saw them flinching "The bastard must have read my mind!"

> **Maxim #992: Anonymous**
>
> We will conserve only what we love. We will love only what we understand. We will understand only what we are taught.

Maxim #993: Anonymous

Wealth is not what we have, but what we are.

Maxim #994: Anonymous

Well the trouble with being a good sport is that you have to lose to prove it.

Maxim #995: Anonymous

What is honored in a country will be cultivated there.

Maxim #996: Anonymous

What is true for you is what you have observed yourself.

Maxim #997: Anonymous

What makes us so bitter against people who outwit us is that they think themselves cleverer than we are.

Maxim #998: Anonymous

What man does not understand, he fears; and what he fears, he tends to destroy.

Maxim #999: Anonymous

What men learn from history is that men do not learn from history.

Maxim #1000: Anonymous

What most people need to learn in life is how to love people and use things instead of using people and loving things.

Maxim #1001: Anonymous

What no spouse of a writer can ever understand is that a writer is working when he's staring out the window.

Maxim #1002: Anonymous

What on earth are you doing for Heaven's sake?

Maxim #1003: Anonymous

What passes for woman's intuition is often nothing more than man's transparency.

Maxim #1004: Anonymous

What this country needs is a good 5 dollar plasma weapon.

Maxim #1005: Anonymous

What three things do you want to accomplish this year? Write them down and place them on your refrigerator for inspiration all year long.

Maxim #1006: Anonymous

What to do with your weight: pull it, don't throw it around.

Maxim #1007: Anonymous

What's good enough for our ancestors is good enough for us.

Maxim #1008: Anonymous

What's so remarkable about Love at first sight? It's when people have been looking at each other for years that it becomes remarkable.

Maxim #1009: Anonymous

Whatever your lot in life, build something on it.

Maxim #1010: Anonymous

Whatever your past has been your future is spotless.

Maxim #1011: Anonymous

When a fellow can't read, he's got to think.

Maxim #1012: Anonymous

When a man boasts about what he'll do tomorrow we like to find out what he did yesterday.

Maxim #1013: Anonymous

When an action has its intended effect, it also has other, unintended, effects.

Maxim #1014: Anonymous

When death overtakes us; all that we have is left to others; all that we are we take with us.

Maxim #1015: Anonymous

When does summertime come to Minnesota, you ask? Well, last year, I think it was a Tuesday.

Maxim #1016: Anonymous

When friends truly forgive us, it is so much easier to forgive ourselves.

Maxim #1017: Anonymous

When he first ran for office, he appealed to the voters: 'I never stole anything in my life. All I ask is a chance.'

Maxim #1018: Anonymous

When in doubt, tell the truth.

Maxim #1019: Anonymous

When it was seen that many of the wicked seemed quite untroubled by evil consciences ... then the idea of future suffering was advanced.

Maxim #1020: Anonymous

When life seems just a dreary grind; and things seem fated to annoy; say something nice to someone else and watch the world light up with joy.

Maxim #1021: Anonymous

When people yearn with all their hearts For just one treasure far away; They close their eyes to countless joys That crowd around them every day.

Maxim #1022: Anonymous

When spring is dancing among the hills, one should not stay in a little dark corner.

Maxim #1023: Anonymous

When the going seems easy, you may be going downhill.

Maxim #1024: Anonymous

When the law is against you, argue the facts. When the facts are against you, argue the law. When both are against you, call the other lawyer names.

Maxim #1025: Anonymous

When things change inside you, things change around you.

Maxim #1026: Anonymous

When things change inside you, things change around you.

Maxim #1027: Anonymous

When two quarrel, both are in the wrong.

Maxim #1028: Anonymous

When we are right we can afford to keep our tempers. When we are wrong, we can't afford not to.

Maxim #1029: Anonymous

When we become aware of our humility, we've lost it.

Maxim #1030: Anonymous

When we don't stand for something we'll fall for anything.

Maxim #1031: Anonymous

When will you realize Vienna waits for you?

Maxim #1032: Anonymous

When you deplore the conditions in the world, ask yourself, am I part of the problem or part of the solution?

Maxim #1033: Anonymous

When you find a job you love, you'll never have to work a day in your life.

Maxim #1034: Anonymous

When you go home, Tell them of us, and say For your tomorrow, We gave our today.

Maxim #1035: Anonymous

When you go out to buy, don't show your silver.

Maxim #1036: Anonymous

When you have a hammer in your hand, everything looks like a nail.

Maxim #1037: Anonymous

When you obey your superior, you instruct your inferior.

Maxim #1038: Anonymous

When you speak badly about others, you are telling who you are yourself.

Maxim #1039: Anonymous

When you try to make an impression, the chances are that is the impression you will make.

Maxim #1040: Anonymous

When you're average, you're just as close to the bottom as you are the top.

Maxim #1041: Anonymous

When you're not allowed to question the Science, it is not Science. It is Propaganda.

Maxim #1042: Anonymous

When you've boxed yourself in, there is no sunshine.

Maxim #1043: Anonymous

When your OUTGO exceeds your INCOME then your UPKEEP will be your DOWNFALL.

Maxim #1044: Anonymous

When your work speaks for itself, don't interrupt.

Maxim #1045: Anonymous

Whenever competent people are not a good fit for your team the problem often lies not with competent people.

Maxim #1046: Anonymous

Whenever two hypotheses cover the facts, use the simpler of the two.

Maxim #1047: Anonymous

Where ambition ends happiness begins.

Maxim #1048: Anonymous

While not all liberals are devils, all devils are.

Maxim #1049: Anonymous

Why does everything have to be so significant? Finding significance in your life doesn't necessarily make you happy.

Maxim #1050: Anonymous

Why is it, that the less that you have to do, the more difficult it is to DO something?

Maxim #1051: Anonymous

Why worry when you can pray?

Maxim #1052: Anonymous

Wise are they who have learned these truths: Trouble is temporary. Time is a tonic. Tribulation is a test tube.

Maxim #1053: Anonymous

Wise men have long ears, big eyes and short tongue.

Maxim #1054: Anonymous

With all the fancy scientists in the world, why can't they just once build a nuclear balm?

Maxim #1055: Anonymous

Without health you cannot enjoy wealth or happiness.

Maxim #1056: Anonymous

Without love intelligence is dangerous; without intelligence love is not enough.

Maxim #1057: Anonymous

Without loving acts, loving words are meaningless.

Maxim #1058: Anonymous

Without order, nothing can grow or expand.

Maxim #1059: Anonymous

Without role models in their life your kids become someone else's dough.

Maxim #1060: Anonymous

Without wind, grass does not move.

Maxim #1061: Anonymous

Without wisdom, knowledge is more stupid than ignorance.

Maxim #1062: Anonymous

Work is love made visible.

Maxim #1063: Anonymous

Worry is today's mice nibbling on tomorrow's cheese.

Maxim #1064: Anonymous

Worry takes as much time as work and pays less.

Maxim #1065: Anonymous

Worry: a sustained form of fear caused by indecision.

Maxim #1066: Anonymous

Yes, but every time I try to see things your way, I get a headache.

Maxim #1067: Anonymous

You amass things only to enjoy them.

Maxim #1068: Anonymous

You are sympathetic and understanding to other people's problems. They think you are a sucker.

Maxim #1069: Anonymous

You are taking advantage of the good nature of a friend. Be careful.

Maxim #1070: Anonymous

You are young at any age if you are planning for tomorrow.

Maxim #1071: Anonymous

You become like those who you idealize, admire and follow.

Maxim #1072: Anonymous

You can always tell a Harvard man, but you can't tell him much.

Maxim #1073: Anonymous

You can fool all of the people all of the time, but why bother when all you need is a simple majority?

Maxim #1074: Anonymous

You can fool some of the conservatives, some of the time.   You will fool most of the liberals, most of the time.   But you can't fool Trump.

Maxim #1075: Anonymous

You can have peace. Or you can have freedom. Never count on having both at once.

Maxim #1076: Anonymous

You can judge a man by what he laughs at.

Maxim #1077: Anonymous

You can no more give what you haven't learned than you can come back from a place you've never been.

Maxim #1078: Anonymous

You can say no and smile only when there's a bigger yes burning inside you

Maxim #1079: Anonymous

You can tell what a man is by what he does when he hasn't anything to do.

Maxim #1080: Anonymous

You can't antagonize and influence at the same time.

Maxim #1081: Anonymous

You can't do it, unless you dream it, first!

Maxim #1082: Anonymous

You can't expect to meet the challenges of today with yesterday's tools and expect to be in business tomorrow.

Maxim #1083: Anonymous

You can't judge a book by the way it wears its hair.

Maxim #1084: Anonymous

You can't make a fact out of an opinion by raising your voice.

Maxim #1085: Anonymous

You can't steal second base and keep your foot on first.

Maxim #1086: Anonymous

You cannot achieve the impossible without attempting the absurd.

Maxim #1087: Anonymous

You cannot build a reputation on the things you are going to do.

Maxim #1088: Anonymous

You cannot further the brotherhood of man by inciting class hatred.

Maxim #1089: Anonymous

You cannot help small men up by tearing down big men.

Maxim #1090: Anonymous

You cannot kill time without injuring eternity.

Maxim #1091: Anonymous

You cannot sit on the road to success for if you do, you will get run over.

Maxim #1092: Anonymous

You cannot succeed by criticising others.

> **Maxim #1093: Anonymous**
>
> You don't know what you don't know, and you don't know you don't know it.

> **Maxim #1094: Anonymous**
>
> You have the capacity to learn from mistakes. You'll learn a lot today.

> **Maxim #1095: Anonymous**
>
> You have the power to think what you want. No matter what the circumstance.

> **Maxim #1096: Anonymous**
>
> You judge your own acts only by their consequences.

Maxim #1097: Anonymous

You keep on getting what you've been getting when you keep on doing what you've been doing.

Maxim #1098: Anonymous

You keep your equilibrium no matter what position you find yourself in.

Maxim #1099: Anonymous

You know how you hate to be interrupted, so why are you always doing it to me.

Maxim #1100: Anonymous

You know it's going to be a bad day when you call suicide prevention and they put you on hold.

Maxim #1101: Anonymous

You know it's going to be a bad day when you see a 60 Minutes news team waiting in your office.

Maxim #1102: Anonymous

You know what to fight for and what to compromise on.

Maxim #1103: Anonymous

You know you're getting old when it takes to much effort to procrastinate.

Maxim #1104: Anonymous

You know you've landed gear-up when it takes full power to taxi.

Maxim #1105: Anonymous

You love what you find time to do.

Maxim #1106: Anonymous

You make a living by what you get, but you make a life by what you give.

Maxim #1107: Anonymous

You may be conservative, cautious and practical.

Maxim #1108: Anonymous

You may be the only standard work somebody ever reads.

Maxim #1109: Anonymous

You respect those superior to yourself and try to learn from them.

Maxim #1110: Anonymous

You will have many friends when you use a corkscrew.

Maxim #1111: Anonymous

You will secure the greatest degree of happiness if you marry young.

Maxim #1112: Anonymous

You would rather be admired than liked, although you would prefer both.

Maxim #1113: Anonymous

You're not what you think you are; you're not what others think you are; you're what you think others think you are!

Maxim #1114: Anonymous

You're on the road to success when you realize that failure is only a detour.

Maxim #1115: Anonymous

Your customers will get better when you do.

Maxim #1116: Anonymous

Your dreams come true when you act to turn them into realities.

Maxim #1117: Anonymous

Your failures won't hurt you until you start blaming them on others.

Maxim #1118: Anonymous

Your future lies ahead of you Like a sheet of fallen snow. Be careful where you take a step Because its sure to show.

Maxim #1119: Anonymous

Your happiness is intertwined with your outlook on life.

Maxim #1120: Anonymous

Your own qualities will help prevent your advancement in the world.

Maxim #1121: Anonymous

Your persistence is your measure of faith in yourself.

Maxim #1122: Anonymous

Your place in the path of life is in the driver's seat.